Our Island Tasmania

Dawn on the Tamar River at Rosevears.

Our Island Tasmania

Photographs and design by Owen Hughes M.Photo. FAIPP
Text by Julian Burgess

'GREEN GABLES'

PUBLISHED & DISTRIBUTED BY OWEN HUGHES

17 Elizabeth Street, Launceston, Tasmania 7250, Australia. Telephone: (03) 6331 1481

http://www.owenhughes.com.au/

First Published 2010

© Copyright 2010: Owen Hughes

All rights reserved. No part of this publication may be reproduced, stored in a retrieval system or transmitted in any form or by any means, electronic, mechanical, photocopying, recording or otherwise, without prior permission of the publisher.

Colour separation of digital images & typesetting by Computer Support Tasmania, Lilydale, Tasmania 7268, Australia

Colour separation of transparencies, printing & binding: Tien Wah Press (PTE) Limited. Printed in Singapore.

National Library of Australia ISBN number: 978-0-9808317-0-2

Wineglass Bay, Freycinet National Park on the East Coast.

FOREWORD

When I was asked to write this foreword, I tried to remember the "one and only" shot that stroked my mind more than any other. "Le Baiser de l'Hotel de Ville", by the French photographer Robert Doisneau, immediately came to mind as this photo is universally known and acclaimed. Like most, I believed it was an inspirational snapshot taken on the spur of the moment in romantic Paris until years later, when Monsieur Doisneau finally admitted that, on the contrary, his photo was a very carefully crafted composition, using professional models. The work of a genuine artisan had touched the whole world, transcending generations and cultures, because behind the picture, the viewer (including me) could dream and imagine the story of this couple in a hurry and in love. This is the kind of photographer Owen Hughes is.

The power of advertising is undeniable. One of the biggest world myths about photography could possibly be an advertising slogan that cradled my earlier years in France. It said, "Clic-Clac merci Kodak" and convinced me and millions of others that taking a photo was the easiest thing in the world and almost anyone could soundly do it. Clic-Clac was an almost perfect (at least in French) phonetic description of the noise made by the then mechanical shutter used in the mass produced cameras. Today, the myth is as strong as ever and we can even take photos with our mobile phones fitted with an artificial fake noise reproducing the famous "Clic-Clac". The reality is that almost all the photos taken by you, others and me, average amateur photographers, dreadfully lack technical soundness and soul.

Strangely enough, some pretty ordinary photos can (and have) become very successful, and some outstanding ones will languish in the darkrooms where they were created; such is the random nature of art. However, there is a big difference between an artist and an artisan. Owen Hughes is an artisan. Every photo that you will find in this book not only tells a thousand words but, like any good book or film, has been carefully and patiently crafted in the good, old-fashioned artisan way, where traditional hard work is preferred to fickle and hypothetical genius. It is for this reason that each photo in this book holds a story behind the picture itself.

I encourage you to take your time looking at them, allowing your mind to wander and glide, and if you show as much patience and keenness as the craftsman who created the images, some of them might even whisper to your soul the "stories" hidden behind them. Tasmania is an enigmatic, personal, precious and multifaceted gem on the planet Earth, and one has to earn its intimacy. Owen's photos will be one of your best possible threads in the journey you are about to commence in your quest to love our island as much as Owen and I do.

Mayor Bertrand CADART.

Glamorgan-Spring Bay Council. 2010.

CONTENTS

Tasmania Generally	2 - 23
Introduction	10 - 11
North & North East	24 - 59
South & South East	60 - 87
North West & West	88 - 111
Map	112

ACKNOWLEDGEMENTS

Special thanks to my wife Marcia for her understanding and patience and to all my family and friends who have offered their help and opinions with the production of this book and to Glamorgan-Spring Bay Mayor Bertrand Cadart for the kind words in his foreword.

Fishing boats at rest in Victoria Dock, Hobart. A hint of mist covers the summit of Mt. Wellington in the background.

An annual display of tulips in Hobart's Royal Tasmanian Botanical Gardens.

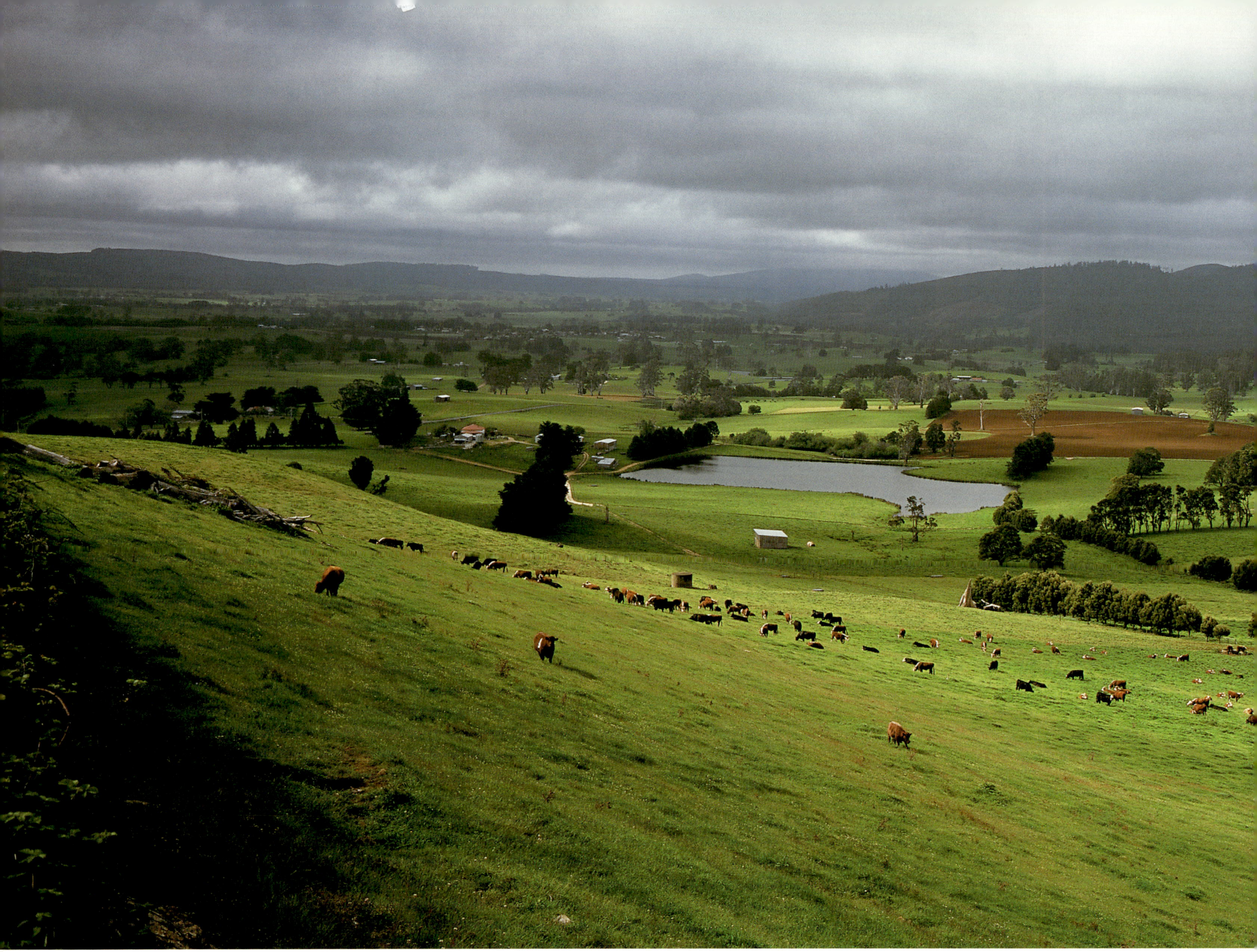

Cattle graze in the lush pastures of the Ringarooma Valley, North East Tasmania.

INTRODUCTION

Tasmania is an island of great beauty and few places in the world can match it for the variety of stunning landscapes. From the brilliant white beaches of the Bay of Fires, to the majestic peaks of Cradle Mountain and the dense rain forests of the rugged South West wilderness it offers outstanding scenery. It combines contemporary living in close proximity to its history and the natural environment. And just about anyone from the casual day tripper to the seasoned adventurer can experience it.

Australia's smallest state lies between latitude 40 and 44 degrees South and is 360 kilometres long and 300 kilometres wide. With 5400 kilometres of coastline, it is the largest of Australia's 8000 islands and the world's 26th biggest island. More than a third of its 68,401 square kilometre landmass, which includes the subantarctic Macquarie Island, is protected in State Reserves, National Parks and World Heritage Areas.

Tasmania's history is as dramatic and diverse as its environment. Its location in the Roaring Forties, where the clean air of the Southern Ocean circulates the globe almost unimpeded, ensures a temperate climate that nurtures unique flora and fauna. But it wasn't always like this. Around 35,000 years ago Tasmania was still connected to mainland Australia by a land bridge across what is now Bass Strait. King and Flinders islands are remnants of that connection.

Over millennia the rising sea levels isolated the environment and its inhabitants. The Tasmanian Aborigines adapted to the often harsh climate and the changing landscape. They developed their own languages and communities and lived in harmony with a land they had all to themselves. That changed on November 24, 1642, when Dutchman Abel Tasman first sighted the formidable West Coast on a voyage of exploration from Batavia (now Jakarta). Two days later his ship anchored on the South East Coast and he planted the Dutch flag. He called the place Van Diemen's Land.

It would be more than a century before Europeans again visited the remote and rugged lands sighted by Tasman. French explorer Marion du Fresne arrived next, in 1772, and then the Englishman Tobias Furneaux, sailing with the great navigator James Cook, landed at South Cape in 1773. British and French expeditions followed to chart the coastline, catalogue the flora and fauna and look for trading opportunities. It wasn't until 1798 that Royal Navy navigator Matthew Flinders and surgeon George Bass, sailing in the sloop Norfolk, established that Van Diemen's Land was separated from the Australian mainland. They bestowed many of the place names in use today.

The voyage of Bass and Flinders paved the way for the British to claim Van Diemen's Land in 1803 and establish a penal colony at what would become Hobart. The North of the island was settled in 1804 with Launceston being established in 1806. Some of the early European visitors thought it was the end of the world but the combination of convict labour and hardworking free settlers saw the rapid development of Van Diemen's Land. Towns sprang up and the colony's midlands quickly became grazing lands for sheep and cattle.

The Moon and Venus set in the west on a clear autumn evening.

In 1835 John Batman left Launceston for Port Phillip Bay and helped establish a settlement on the Yarra River that would become Melbourne. Hardy woodsmen cleared the dense forests of the island's North West Coast to create farmlands and were soon supplying timber to the growing communities of Victoria and beyond.

Traders and fishermen used the Tamar and Mersey rivers as bases for their voyages across Bass Strait and to the many islands between the North Coast and mainland Australia. After 50 years of settlement the people of Van Diemen's Land were ready to take charge of their own affairs. After much agitating, convict transportation ended in 1853 and in 1856 the island was officially named Tasmania and elected its first parliament.

By 1900 the island had become an important producer of wool, timber and minerals with a population of 100,000. Its residents were a driving force in the move to the federation of Australian states. World wars and military conflicts of the last century saw Tasmanians serving their country overseas. After these conflicts there was a surge of immigration from war-ravaged parts of Europe and Asia that helped to create a multicultural society.

In the 21st Century, Tasmania is home to about 500,000 people with nearly half the population living in Hobart, more than 100,000 people living in Launceston and the Tamar Valley and 70,000 living along the North West and West Coasts. Timber and minerals are still important resources but fruit and vegetables, meat, dairy products, seafoods, wine and beers have become valuable exports. Craftsmen and women turn the island's unique timbers, metals, glass and clays into works of art. Tourism is a major industry.

Perhaps because of their relative isolation Tasmanians often display a high level of innovation and enterprise. This is evident in the development of high-tech ships, mining equipment, aquaculture and computer software. And Tasmania is home to major sporting and social events, hosting Test Cricket at Hobart's Bellerive Oval, Australian Rules Football at Launceston's Aurora Stadium and innovative events like Targa Tasmania, the Taste of Tasmania and Festivale.

Performances by the Tasmanian Symphony Orchestra, vineyard concerts with international performers like Tom Jones and the Falls Festival at Marion Bay all provide world class entertainment to residents and visitors alike.

Tasmania's isolation has ensured that much of its natural environment is unspoilt and its Aboriginal heritage has survived. Many of the colonial homes, government and commercial buildings and structures remain to complement the island's modern, vibrant lifestyle. The images in this book are proof that Tasmania is an island of diversity and wonder.

Hibbertia flowers during spring in the Winifred Curtis Reserve near Scamander.

Evandale near Launceston Airport awakes to a misty autumn morning.

A large crowd is entertained by international artist Tom Jones at Josef Chromy vineyards in Relbia Road, near Launceston.

Terns take a rest while a dramatic spring shower passes over Scamander barway on the East Coast.

Early morning pastoral scene at Westbury, with Quamby Bluff in the background.

The Hellyer River floods through the dense rainforest of the North West.

The winding and hilly terrain between Launceston and Scottsdale is perfect for the Sideling section of Targa Tasmania held each year in April.

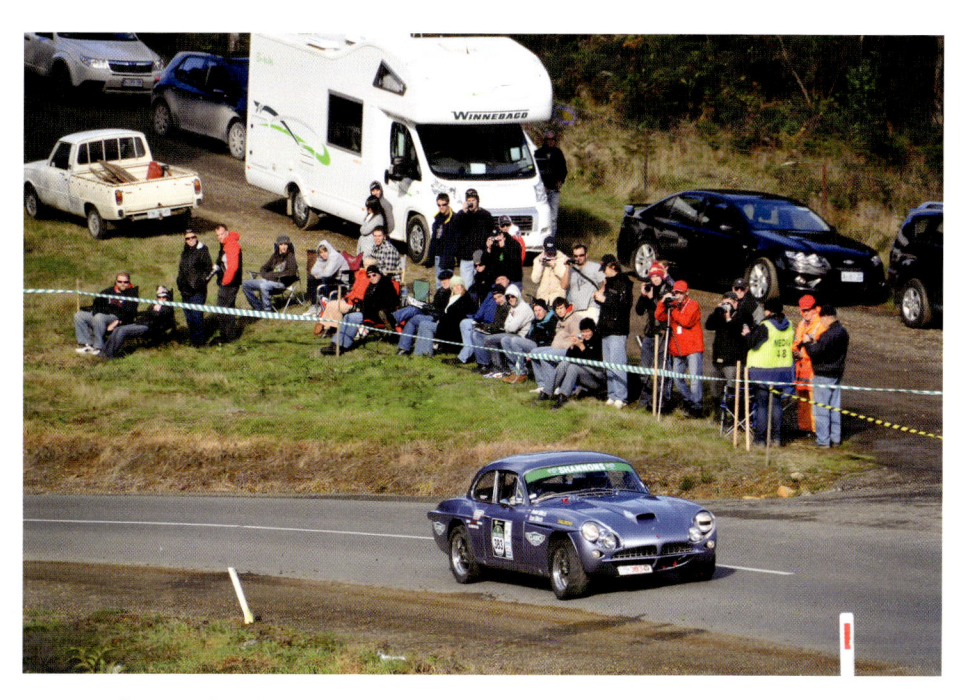

Car enthusiasts gather at vantage points along the course.

Jason White of Burnie was the overall winner in his Lamborghini in 2010.

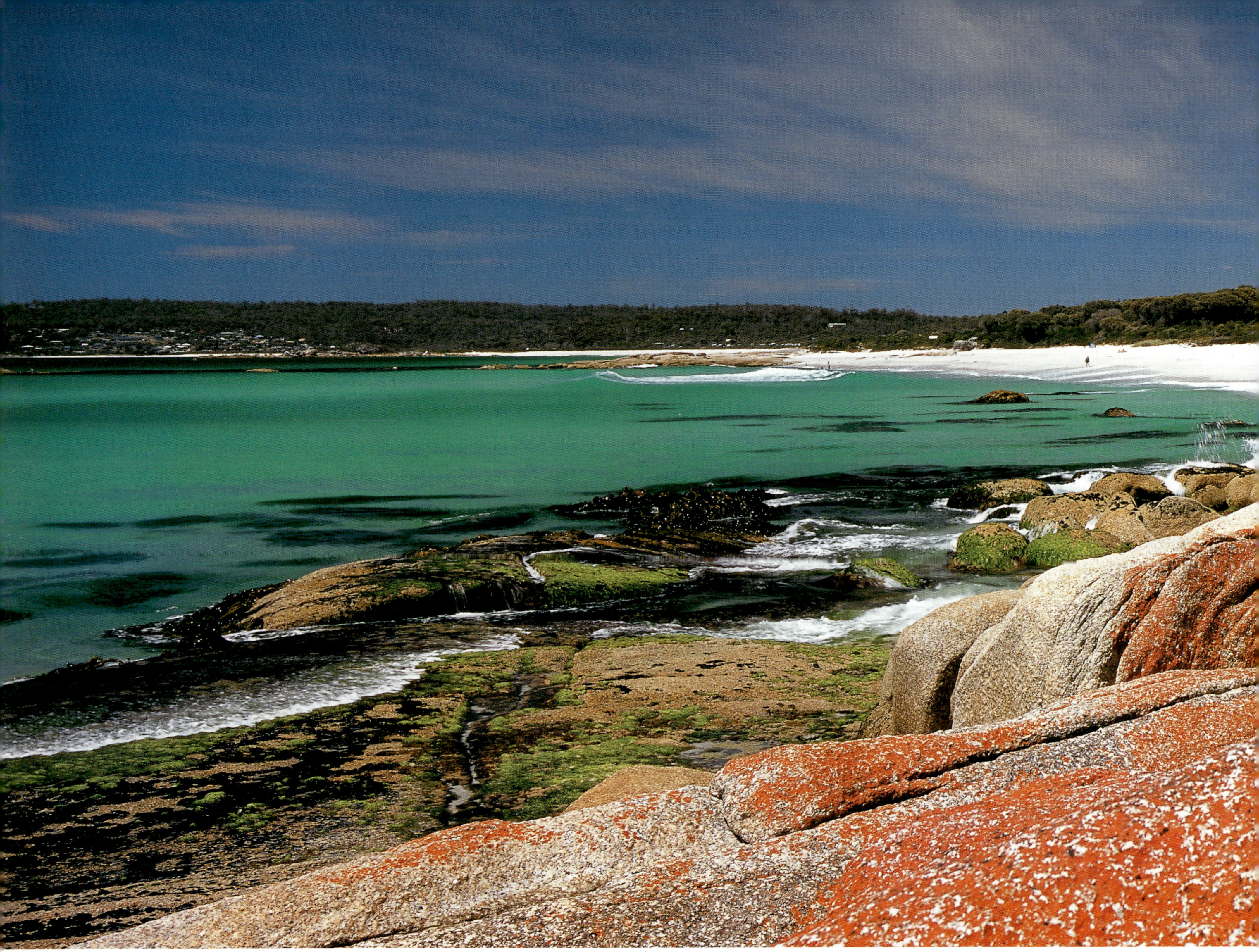

Cosy Corner in the Bay of Fires Reserve on Tasmania's North East Coast is popular with campers during the summer months. The Bay of Fires was judged as the world's hottest travel destination in 2009 by Lonely Planet magazine.

Former Miss Universe, Laura Dundovic, Women's classic race wear winner, Eliza Pitt from Hobart and Mark Brown of Launceston.

Fashions on show at Mowbray Race Course on Launceston Cup Day in February.

Australian Test Cricket Captain, Launceston born Ricky Ponting displays his form at Bellerive Oval.

Ricky made his Test cricket debut at the age of 20 and has been Australian Test cricket captain since 2004.

Photo: Paul Scambler.

Priestly Glacier in Antarctica. This photo was taken on the inaugural A380 scenic flight at about 1.30 am. on the first of January, 2010.

Tasmania is not a part of Antarctica but much of our weather is generated from the Antarctic region.

The popular Falls Festival at Marion Bay. Maria Island can be seen in the distance.

Early morning fog in the valley near Carrick with miniature 'mountain waves' forming over the tree tops in the right hand corner.

NORTH & NORTH EAST

The centre of Launceston is only minutes from the spectacular Cataract Gorge reserve and provides a dramatic connection between a large, modern regional city and the beauty of the Tasmanian countryside. In summer it is a peaceful refuge but when the winter rains send floodwaters down the South Esk River there are few more awesome sights. Launceston sits at the head of the beautiful Tamar Valley and is home to many Georgian buildings, regional businesses and local industries. The imposing Customs House on the North Esk River sits near the historic J. Boag and Son brewery. The Queen Victorian Museum and Art Gallery holds some of Australia's most important colonial artworks.

The region is home to several major events. The Hawthorn Football Club has made Launceston's Aurora Stadium its Tasmanian home and the city hosts the start of the Targa Tasmania tarmac rally. Nearby Evandale stages the annual penny-farthing championships. Festivale, a celebration of Tasmanian food and wine, is held in Launceston's City Park each February and attracts more than 40,000 people. The Launceston Cup is the state's biggest race meeting, Agfest at Carrick is one of the largest agricultural events in the country and the V8 Supercars race at Symmons Plains each year.

In winter the snow fields of Ben Lomond provide skiing for locals and visitors while the many vineyards on the banks of the Tamar River estuary grow world-class wines. The outstanding restaurants in the region draw their produce from the many orchards and berry farms in the valley. At George Town the region's maritime history is on show at the Norfolk Museum and the Low Head Pilot Station.

At Beaconsfield's working gold mine there are reminders of Tasmania's gold rush days and to the east the remains of the state's tin mining industry can be seen at Derby, Gladstone and on the Blue Tier. St Helens, set on beautiful Georges Bay, is the state's home of game fishing and hosts charter boats and a commercial fishing fleet. To the north the spectacular, untouched white beaches of the Bay of Fires have become an international attraction. The red-stained granite rocks along the coastline provide a brilliant contrast for the many holiday-makers who flock to the area.

The farms and coastal waters of Northern Tasmania provide a rich bounty in food from the land and the sea. Scottsdale is famous for its potatoes and its forestry and Pyengana for its dairy products. The fishing towns of Bridport, St Helens and Bicheno provide lobster, scallops and oysters as well as scale fish.

The North is dotted with colonial villages. In Evandale, Longford, Westbury and Deloraine much of the early architecture remains. And on the Heritage Highway the history of the island has been well preserved and is clearly visible in the churches, homes and buildings of Campbell Town and Ross. There is so much to see and do.

Beauty Point on the western banks of the Tamar River.

Historic buildings in Elizabeth Street, Launceston.

Launceston's oldest dwelling.   Painted pole at Lilydale    Launceston Town Clock. 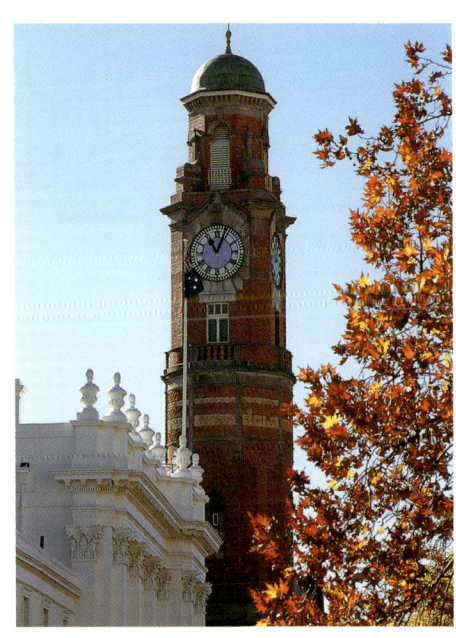   Carrick Mill and restaurant.

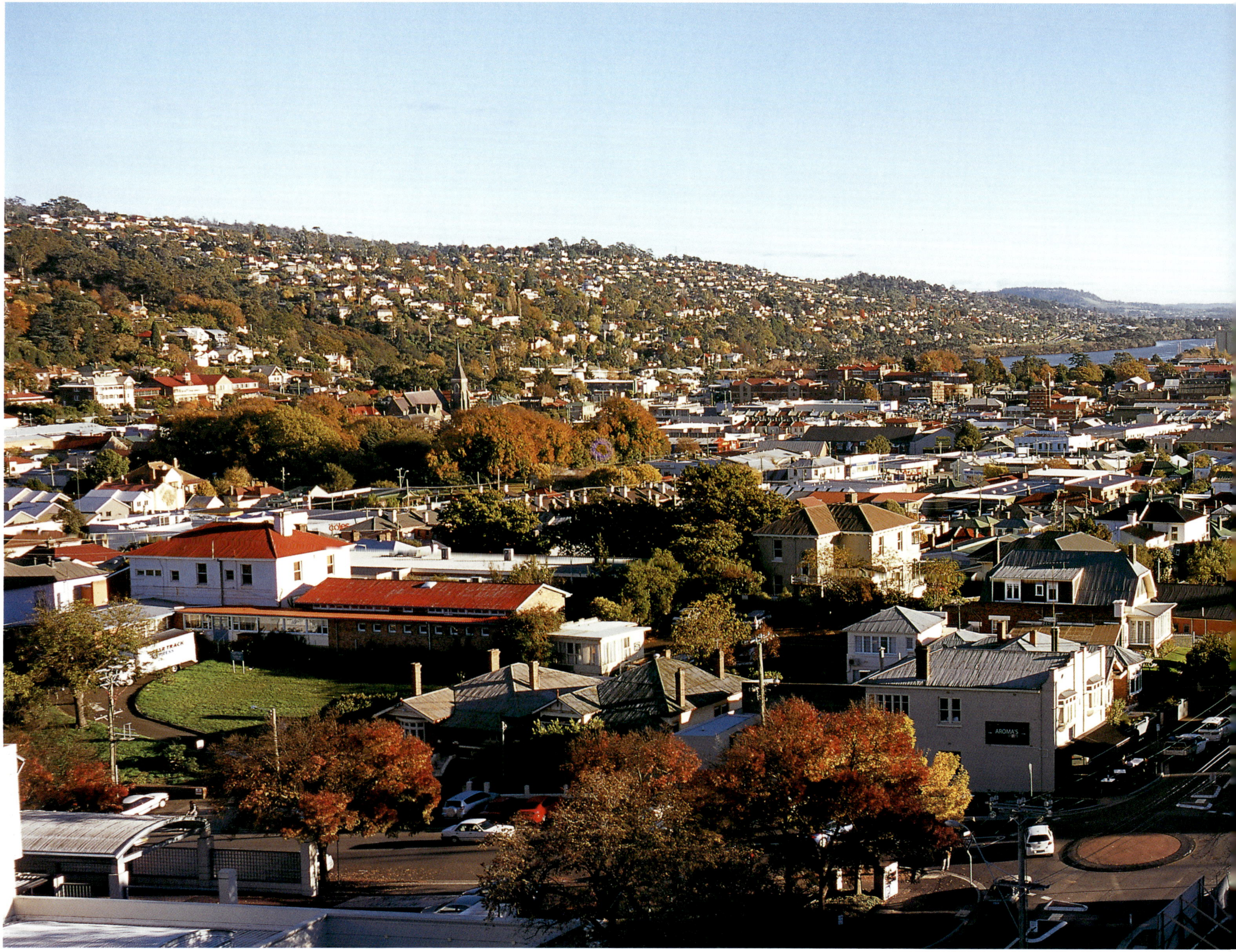
AROMA'S

Panoramic view of Launceston from the new luxury penthouse suite on top of the old Launceston general hospital building.

'Festivale', a music, food and wine festival held each February in Launceston's City Park.

The thundering turbulence of the South Esk River as it floods through Cataract Gorge.

Misty light on the suspension bridge at the First Basin in Launceston's Cataract Gorge.

The summer scene at the swimming pool at the First Basin in the Cataract Gorge.

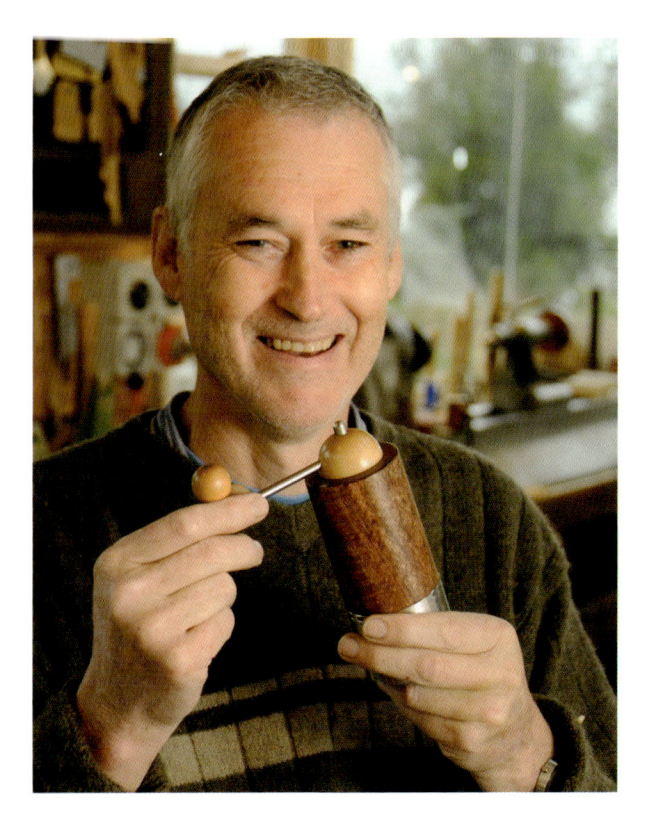

Patrick Senior of Indeco value adding Tasmanian timbers.

Show and Shine at Richardson's Harley Davidson

Ron Murray gives a shearing demonstration at Agfest.

Aerial view of the vineyards and wineries along the banks of the Tamar River at Rosevears.

The historic bridge built in 1836 at Ross in the midlands.

Talented chainsaw artist Bill Freeman at work at Campbell Town.

Brisbane Street Mall, Launceston.

Re-enactment of yesteryear at Evandale.

Penny Farthing races which are held at Evandale each February.

Car talk between Kelvin Campbell and Greg Stone at Woolmers during the Australian A Model Ford car rally.

Autumn reflections of Woolmers Estate in the Macquarie River at Longford.

George Town near the mouth of the Tamar River with historic Low Head pilot station and light house in the background.

A free range wallaby and peacock feed quietly together at the cliff grounds, Cataract Gorge.

The Hydro Tasmania Wild Water World Cup contestants in action in Cataract Gorge in 2009.

Photo: Henry Watts.

A rainbow forms in the fog at Cleveland in the northern midlands.

Forester kangaroos in the evening light at Narawntapu National Park.

Derelict truck at Mangana.

A wombat near his burrow at Narawntapu National Park.

Winter at Upper Blessington on the northern slopes of Ben Lomond.

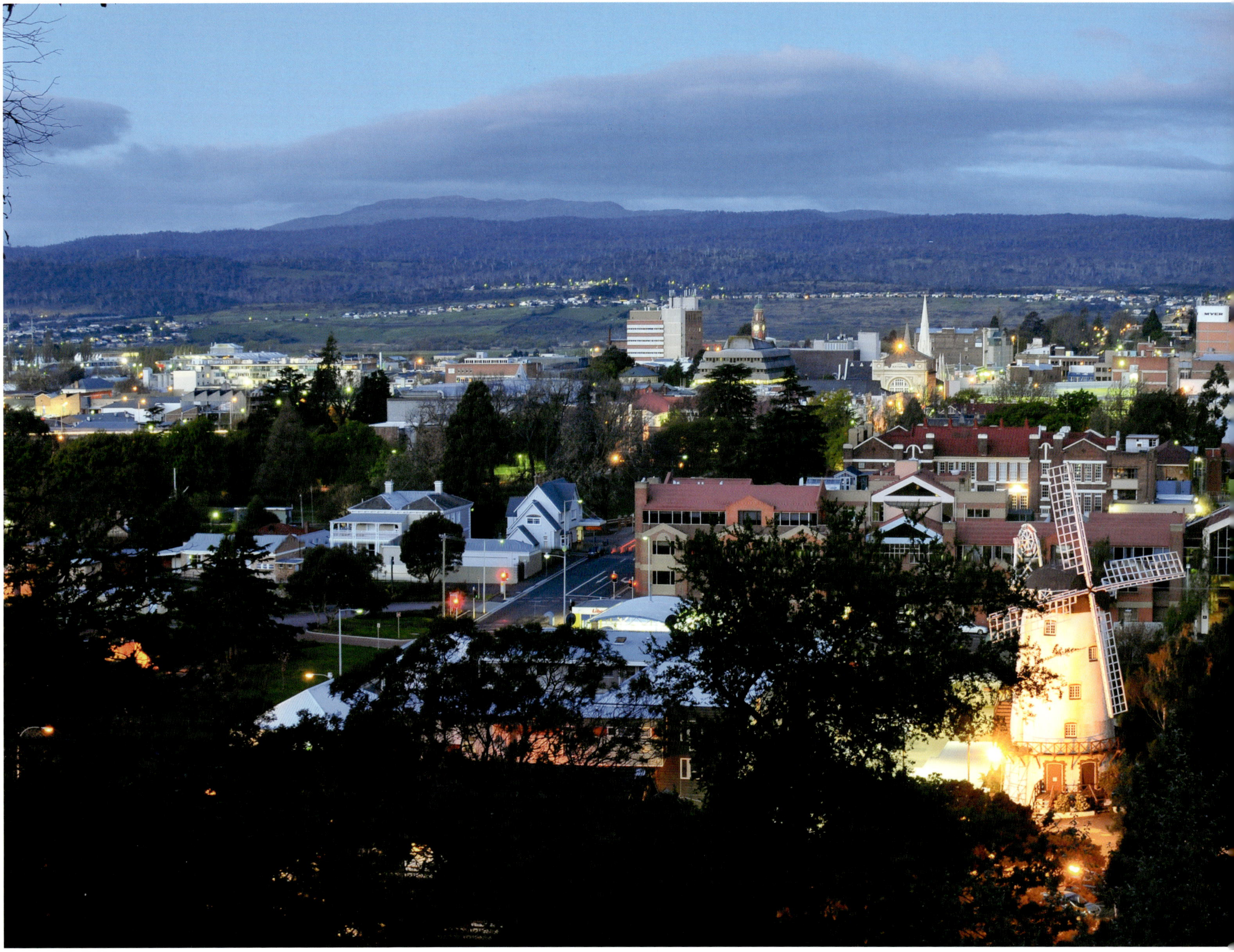

Evening panoramic view of Launceston city as the full moon rises over Mt. Barrow.

Light mist drifts through the long shadows of a late autumn sunrise near Evandale.

Son-in-law Steven, a keen photographer, photographs the summer wild flowers on Ben Lomond, about one hours drive from Launceston.

Launceston City Park first established in 1841.

Evening at the Seaport resort in Launceston.

'Lady Launceston' tourist boat in Cataract Gorge.

Aerial view of Launceston central city.

Launceston College production 'Back to the 80s' at the Princess Theatre.

Before their Anzac Day clash at Launceston's Aurora Stadium players from Hawthorn and North Melbourne stand to attention with the Australian flag at half-mast as they listen to the Last Post. Photo: Will Swan

Action at Aurora Stadium during a daytime match between the Tassie Hawks and the Adelaide Crows.

Moonlight over the Tamar River at Beauty Point.

Love in the swamp. During mating dragon flies fly united when moving from one spot to another.

Large paddocks of canola are grown in Tasmania, like this one on Benham Estate at Avoca. Ben Lomond is in the background.

Ben Lomond ski village is popular during winter, but in recent years the seasons have been mostly very short due to a lack of snow.

An aerial view of the rich farmlands of the Scottsdale region in Tasmania's North East.

Whitemark on Flinders Island, with Mt. Strzelecki in the background.

Goose Island, part of the Furneaux group catches the westerly gales of Bass Strait.

Swan Island which is not far off the North East coast of Tasmania.

Typical rainforest country near St Columba Falls.

Trigger plants grow on the steep slopes of Elephant Pass in iron bark country.

St Columba Falls, a popular tourist attraction not far from the famous "Pub in the Paddock' and the Pyengana Dairy Company.

Surf fishing as the full moon rises over Lagoons Beach on the East Coast.

The utter devastation of the Scamander bushfires in 2006.

Colourful seed pods form after the following years' growth.

Echidnas return when new growth forms.

A black cockatoo returns to hunt for grubs in the trees.

The revival of coastal bushland at Winifred Curtis Reserve near Scamander after being devastated by the bushfires of 2006.

Rick Lohrey catches a trout in the upper reaches of the South Esk River while Steven Jurgoit looks on.

Young Tasmanian Devils in a playful mood in the hands of carer Andrew Pottage at East Coast Nature World near Bicheno.

Ian Summers of St Marys is an avid collector of all things old.

Holiday makers gather on the white sands at Binalong Bay in the Bay of Fires Coastal Reserve during the Christmas, New Year break.

Clouds colour crimson over Cod Rock at Bicheno.

East Coast farmer Brian Hughes, drives a small flock of fine wool Merino sheep at Bicheno.

A surfer catches a wave at Four Mile Creek.

Launceston artist Brian Mooney paints the scene at Waubs Bay, Bicheno, while crowds gather for the 'Devil of a Swim' competition.

SOUTH & SOUTH EAST

Hobart's waterfront is testament to the city's origins as Tasmania's first settlement, the seat of colonial government and its history as a whaling and trading port in the days of sail. With the imposing Mt Wellington as a backdrop, it is Australia's second oldest capital city (after Sydney) and reminders of its early days are everywhere.

Today Hobart retains its maritime links but instead of cargo ships it is luxury cruise liners bringing thousands of tourists to what was once considered to be the edge of the world. The port is also home to the Australian Antarctic Division and hosts exploration and research ships heading to the ice each summer.

Every year the finish of the world famous Sydney to Hobart Yacht Race and the food and wine festival Taste of Tasmania in January turn the Hobart waterfront into a big party. The city's vibrant central business district and numerous historic buildings, many dating from the early 1800s, provide a stunning setting to the festivities.

Government House, the Cascade Brewery and Parliament House date from Tasmania's early days and the old buildings of Salamanca Place that once housed maritime merchants and traders today are home to galleries, antique and craft shops, pubs and cafes. Every Saturday the famous Salamanca Market attracts hundreds of shoppers. Within easy reach of Hobart are the towns of Huonville, New Norfolk, Oatlands and Sorell, each with its own story to tell of past and present life in Tasmania.

The beach-side suburbs of Kingston, Tranmere and Blackmans Bay give way to holiday resorts and fishing villages as the River Derwent runs down to the well-named Storm Bay and connects Hobart to the stunning scenery of Bruny Island and the D'Entrecasteaux Channel.

To the west of Hobart is the rugged and almost impenetrable South West National Park which covers more than 600,000 hectares of alpine wilderness. More than 150 kilometres of walking tracks, from Cockle Creek at Recherche Bay to Scotts Peak near Lake Pedder, lie in wait for the experienced and well-prepared bushwalker. For the less adventurous there are daily scenic flights from Hobart Airport to remote Port Davey, over Federation Peak and the Hartz Mountains.

To the east of Hobart is historic Richmond, in the fertile Coal Valley, with the country's oldest bridge (built in 1823) and more examples of Tasmania's rich colonial heritage. Port Arthur, on the Tasman Peninsula, is a living reminder of Tasmania's darker days and origins as a penal colony. Its many sandstone buildings are important parts of Australia's built heritage. The high dolerite cliffs of Tasman Island and surrounding coastline provide images of grandeur and beauty.

Further north Maria Island and the Freycinet National Park, which contains the acclaimed Wineglass Bay, offer more spectacular scenery. Fishing, farming and holiday making are the attractions in the coastal towns of Orford, Swansea and Coles Bay. Along the way there are boutique vineyards offering quality wines.

Marion Bay.

Aerial view of Hobart city looking south towards the mouth of the River Derwent.

An aerial view of Government House in the centre foreground and the Royal Tasmanian Botanical Gardens to the right with Hobart City behind. The Tasman Highway and the River Derwent are on the left.

Large crowds gather at Salamanca Market each Saturday.

The Taste of Tasmania is a real crowd pleaser on Princes Wharf between Christmas and New Year.

Galleries, restaurants and pubs now occupy the original warehouses in Salamanca Place.

Historic homes line Hampden Road in Battery Point. A wisp of cloud gathers on Mt. Wellington in the background.

St David's Park is adjacent to Salamanca Market.

Early morning at Hobart's Victoria Dock. Mure's famous seafood restaurant is on the left.

A quiet scene in Hampden Road in historic Battery Point.

Lunchtime in Salamanca Square.

Busker, Ian Murtagh, entertains lunchtime shoppers in Elizabeth Street Mall.

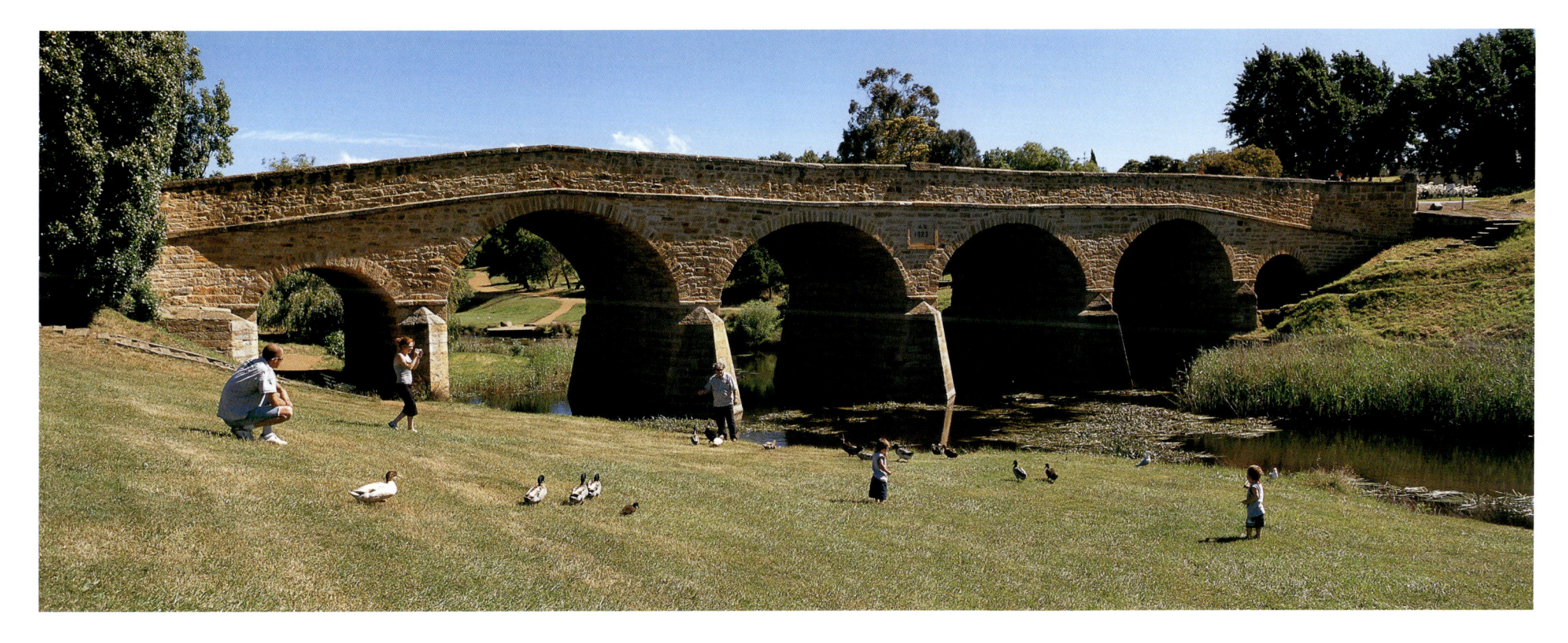

About 30 minutes drive from Hobart is the site of Australia's oldest bridge at Richmond.

Apple blossom in the picturesque Huon Valley.

Sunrise at the Tessellated Pavements, a natural phenomenon at Eaglehawk Neck on the Tasman Peninsula.

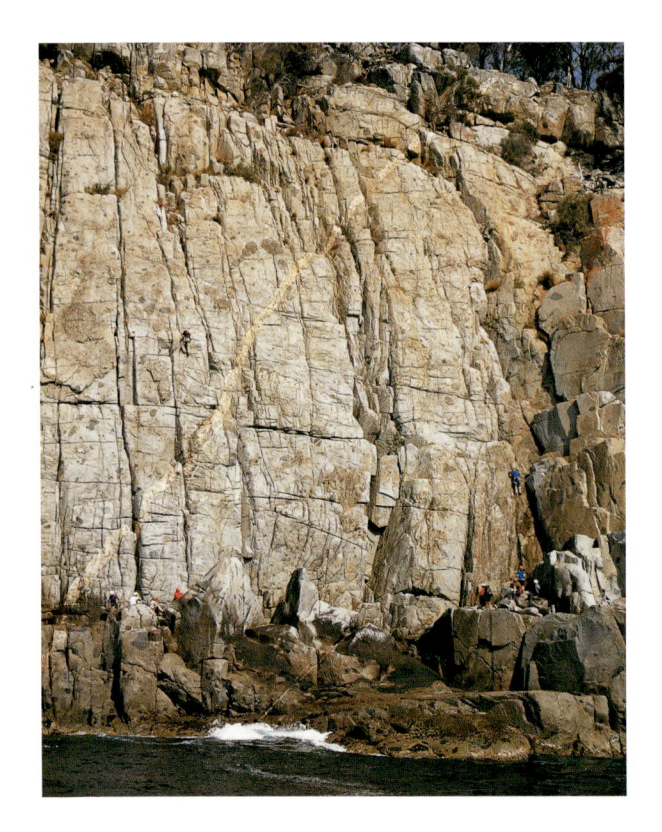

Rock climbing at Bluestone Bay.

Cock Scarlet Robin.

The old boatshed at Kelvedon Beach.

Pirates Bay at Eaglehawk Neck on the Tasman Peninsula is a popular game fishing and holiday area.

An aerial view of historic site, Port Arthur.

Scenic tour boats cut a wake around the base of spectacular 500 metre high cliffs near Cape Pillar.

A stiff north-east breeze fills the spinnaker of a yacht in the Sydney to Hobart ocean race as it rounds Tasman Island.

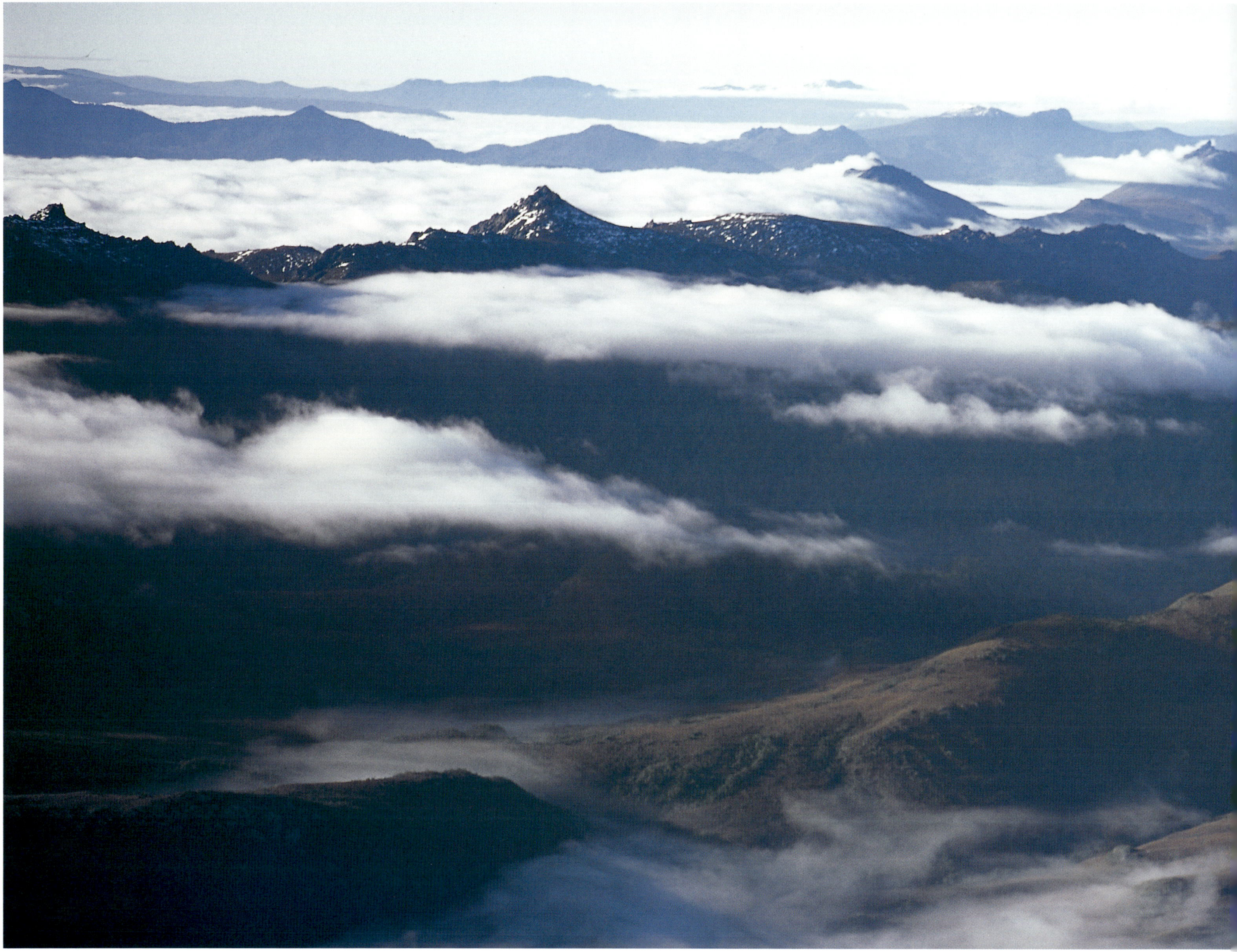

Mist fills the valleys of the vast South-West National Park.

The Coal Valley is typical of the landscape in the lower midlands of Tasmania.

The midlands town of Oatlands boasts a wide range of historic buildings including the Callington Mill dating back to 1836.

Opossum Bay on South Arm is popular with beach lovers.

Reeds Peak and Lake Rhona in the Denison Range are situated west of the Gordon River before it enters Lake Gordon.

Russell Falls in the Mt. Field National Park.

A frosty morning in the Huon Valley.

A welcome wave from colourful identity, Glamorgan – Spring Bay Council Mayor, Bertrand Cadart with his official mayoral vehicle.

This stunning view of Wineglass Bay in the Freycinet National Park is about 30 minutes walk from the car park at Coles Bay.

Freycinet Lodge at Coles Bay sits at the base of The Hazards in the beautiful setting of the national park.

The crystal waters of Wineglass Bay in Freycinet National Park.

The holiday town of Swanwick in the foreground sits at the entrance to the Swan River. At the top left is the township of Coles Bay with The Hazards mountains in Freycinet National Park behind.

The winding Tasman Highway south of Swansea, is great for motor cyclists.

The Hazards form the background to Richardson's Beach at Coles Bay.

The Painted Cliffs on Maria Island National Park.

Dew settles on a spider's web in a honeysuckle tree.

Kangaroo tail plants flower in spring after a bushfire the previous summer.

An aerial view of wetland patterns at the southern end of Moulting Lagoon.

NORTH WEST & WEST

The North West and West Coast regions of Tasmania offer a widely diverse range of images, from the rolling farmlands of Sassafras, to the fishing cottages of Stanley and the stark hills of Queenstown. Along the way there's the iconic Cradle Mountain, numerous sandy beaches between Devonport and Smithton and the haunting beauty of Strahan. It is easy to see why so many people are attracted to this part of Tasmania.

The coastline on Bass Strait is dominated by the geological features of Devonport's Mersey Bluff, Table Cape at Wynyard and The Nut at Stanley. Inland there is an almost endless vista of rugged mountains and forests that contain unique natural features like the Meander Falls and the well-named Crater Lake.

While it was timber for the growing city of Melbourne that drew some early settlers to the region, it is the rich chocolate soils behind Devonport, Ulverstone, Burnie and Smithton that produce potatoes, onions, peas and poppies for local processing factories and interstate and overseas markets.

Devonport is home to the daily Spirit of Tasmania passenger ferry service to Melbourne and the departure port for much of the produce grown in the region. At Sheffield the majestic Mt Roland watches over the annual Muralfest that has turned the town into a gallery of big artworks.

Further west the Leven River runs through the town of Ulverstone which is a busy business centre, holiday resort and a popular place for retirees. Burnie, once home to a major paper manufacturing industry, has reinvented itself as a container and cruise ship port and regional shopping centre. Picturesque Wynyard celebrates the brilliant blooms of the tulip fields on Table Cape with an annual festival and Boat Harbour is famous for its flat, white beach.

The historic fishing village of Stanley is a step back in time with its fishermen's cottages, the Highfield House historic site and Joseph Lyons Cottage, the birthplace of the only Tasmanian Prime Minister of Australia. The chairlift to the top of The Nut provides stunning views of Bass Strait, moored fishing boats and the surrounding coastline.

At the furthest western point of Tasmania, the Cape Grim weather station monitors the cleanest air in the world and the big waves at Marawah, unimpeded by land for thousands of miles, attract surfers from all over the world. The towers of Tasmania's first wind farm are reminders of the powerful winds that sweep up from the Southern Ocean.

The road to the rugged West Coast winds through the Hellyer Gorge on its way to Queenstown where a century of copper mining and smelting has visibly altered the surrounding landscape. Not far away Strahan is a contrast, surrounded by rainforest and with the daunting Hells Gates at the mouth of Macquarie Harbour. Cruise boats line the Strahan waterfront ready to take visitors up the breathtaking Gordon River to experience the unique World Heritage wilderness of Tasmania.

A Currawong in Cradle Mt.– Lake St Clair National Park.

Table Cape near Wynyard is well known for it's rich chocolate soil and many types of crops including tulips.

Crater Lake boat shed set among the autumn colours of deciduous beech (Nothofagus gunnii)*, usually called Fagus.*

Visitors have a great view of Cradle Mountain while standing on Glacier Rock which is only about 300 metres from the car park.

Tulips create a kaleidoscope of colours at Boat Harbour.

A patchwork of paddocks over farmlands west of Devonport. A wide variety of crops are grown including potatoes, carrots and pyrethrum.

A rare dusting of snow on Mt. Roland near the mural and farming town of Sheffield.

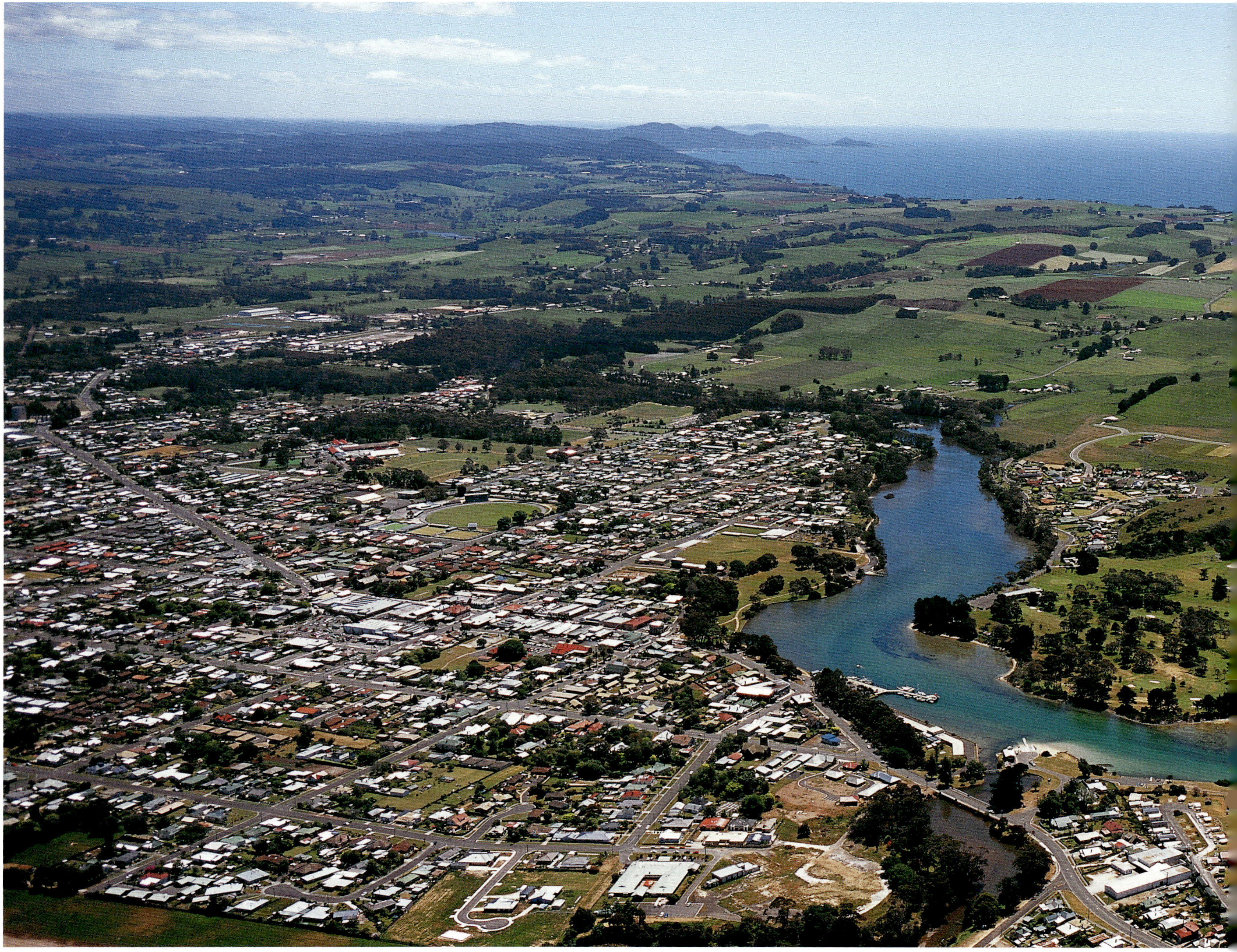

Wynyard at the mouth of the Inglis River is nestled among the rich farming lands of Table Cape. The tulip festival is held here each spring.

Dairying country at Christmas Hills near Deloraine.

The Burnie Ten is held each spring.

Photo. Examiner newspaper

An aerial view of the western suburbs of Burnie, with Somerset in the foreground, then Camdale, Ocean Vista and Cooee.

The cruise ship Dawn Princess leaves the Port of Burnie. Seventeen cruise ships visited Burnie in the 2009-10 summer season.

Rick Rockliff checks his crop of poppies at Sassafras. Tasmania is the only place in the southern hemisphere where opium poppies are grown for legal alkaloid production.

Tasmania is known world wide for its many varieties of berry and stone fruits which are grown throughout the state.

Many vegetable crops are grown in the rich chocolate soil, like this crop of onions.

The Bluff marks the entrance to the Mersey River at Devonport. The Bass Strait ferries, Spirit of Tasmania I and II berth here each day.

The historic fishing, farming and tourist town of Stanley nestles at the base of The Nut.

The Cenotaph and historic buildings at Stanley.

A Wedge-tail Eagle sits alert in the rainforest.

Silver wattles flower in the spring along the banks of the Forth River.

Dawn light on the peaks of Mt. Geryon in the Cradle Mt. – Lake St Clair National Park.

The holiday town of Boat Harbour Beach. Rocky Cape is in the distance.

The township of Ulverstone is situated on the Leven River.

The Murchison Highway winds through the rainforest of Hellyer Gorge.

Fresh winter snow in Weindorfer's Forest, Cradle Mt.

The picturesque Dip Falls on the northern fringes of the Tarkine wilderness area.

Mt. Olympus reflected in the Narcissus River at the top end of Lake St Clair.

A wide range of beautiful ferns grow in the Tasmanian rainforest.

Snow gum in the Cradle Mt. – Lake St Clair National Park.

Spectacular Meander Falls in the Great Western Tiers are about a three hour walk from the car park.

Frenchman's Cap, 1444 metres, is in the Franklin-Gordon Wild Rivers National Park.

World Heritage Cruises vessel 'The Adventurer' tows 114 skiers to set a new world record for the most skiers behind a single boat on Macquarie Harbour at Strahan in March, 2010. Photo: Mark Seaton

Tourists explore the rain forest wilderness of the remote west coast aboard the 32 metre Gordon River Cruises vessel, 'Lady Jane Franklin II'.

A Roaring Forties gale creates huge swells along the rugged West coast of Tasmania.

The Lyell Highway winds through the bare hills between Gormanston and Queenstown.

TASMANIA

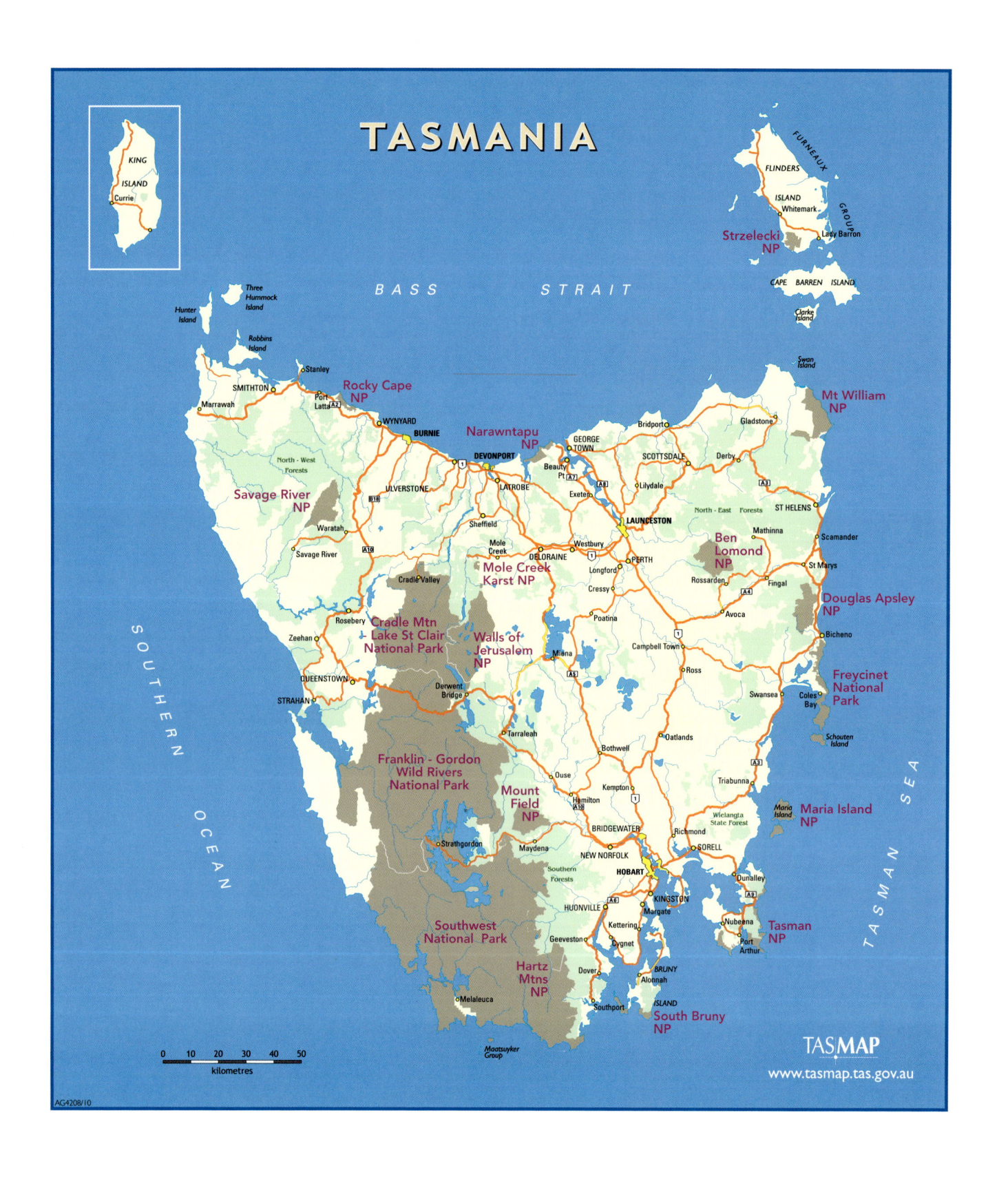